Gus Gets Stuck

By Sally Cowan

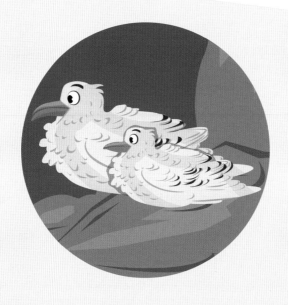

Gus the gull sat on a cliff with his father.

It was not hot.

Dad puffs up his long feathers.

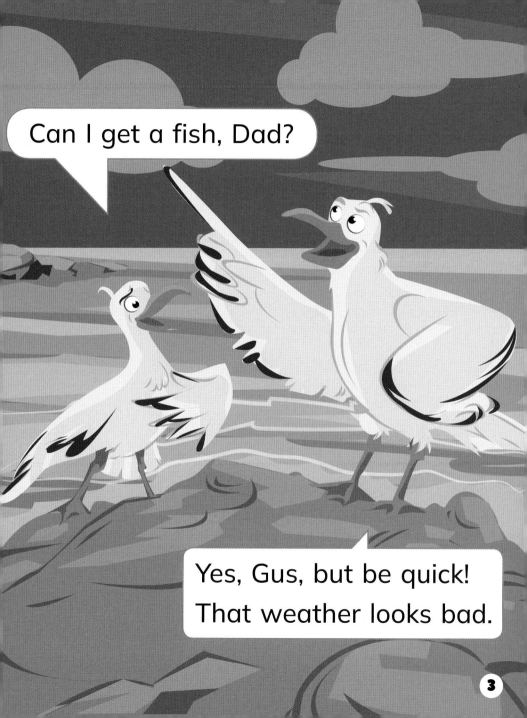

Gus did a quick dip
to get a fish.

But his wings picked up
a net!

Gus rips at the net
with his bill!

But Gus can not get that net
off his long feathers!

The weather is bad,
and Gus is tossed up.

His father tugs and tugs
at the net, but he can not
get it off Gus.

Then, Gus had some luck!

He got tossed on to
the rocks.

Josh was on the rocks
with Beth.

"Look at this little gull!"
said Josh.

Beth got a cloth
and picked Gus up.

"The vet can cut this net
off its feathers," said Josh.
"Let's go!"

CHECKING FOR MEANING

1. What happened to Gus when he went to get a fish? *(Literal)*

2. Who picked Gus up in a cloth? *(Literal)*

3. Why did Dad tell Gus to be quick when the weather looked bad? *(Inferential)*

EXTENDING VOCABULARY

feathers	What are *feathers?* Which animals have feathers? Why do they have them?
picked	What does *picked* mean in this story? How does adding *–ed* to *pick* change the meaning of the base?
luck	Which events in the story show *good luck* and which show *bad luck?*

MOVING BEYOND THE TEXT

1. What bits of rubbish in the ocean can be harmful to birds and fish?

2. How does this rubbish get into the seas and oceans?

3. What might have happened to Gus if the net couldn't be cut off?

4. What are safe ways to pick up stray or injured animals?

SPEED SOUNDS

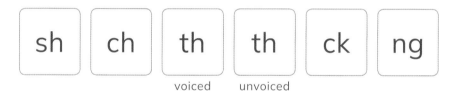

| sh | ch | th | th | ck | ng |

voiced   unvoiced

PRACTICE WORDS

long

with

fish

wings

quick

picked

cloth

luck

rocks

Josh

Beth